Rivka Hadary

FOCUS ON

ISRAEL

Hamish Hamilton · London

For Amnon and Gefen, Avram,
Erez, Dikla,
Smadar, Ammiel,
Hiam, Oren

The author and publisher would like to thank the following for permission to reproduce photographs: Britain/Israel Public Affairs Committee (BIPAC) 9 (left, Klaus Otto-Hundt), 12, 13, 16 (Adam Greene), 17 (right), 18, 20, 21, 22 (right, Netta Saraph), 23 (Netta Saraph), 27, 28 (left), 31; Ralph Goldman 10 (right), 17 (left); Robert Harding Picture Library Ltd 6 (above), 24, 26 (left), 30; Alan Hutchison Picture Library contents page, 6 (below), 7, 8, 10 (left), 14, 19, 22 (left), 25 (below), 26 (right), 29; Israel Colour Slides Co. 28 (right); Tony Stone Associates 11, 15, 25 (above); ZIFA cover and title page.

Map by Janos Marffy

Illustrations by Sara Silcock

Design by Andrew Shoolbred

HAMISH HAMILTON CHILDREN'S BOOKS

Published by the Penguin Group
27 Wrights Lane, London W8 5TZ, England
Viking Penguin Inc., 40 West 23rd Street, New York, New York 10010, U.S.A.
Penguin Books Australia Ltd, Ringwood, Victoria, Australia
Penguin Books Canada Ltd, 2801 John Street, Markham, Ontario, Canada L3R 1B4
Penguin Books (N.Z.) Ltd, 182–190 Wairau Road, Auckland 10, New Zealand

Penguin Books Ltd, Registered Offices: Harmondsworth, Middlesex, England

First published in Great Britain 1988 by
Hamish Hamilton Children's Books

British Library Cataloguing in Publication Data
Hadary, Rivka
Focus on Israel.
1. Israel—Social life and customs.
—Juvenile literature
I. Title
956.94'054 DS112

ISBN 0-241-12091-8

Typeset by Katerprint Typesetting Services, Oxford
Printed in Great Britain by Cambus Litho, East Kilbride

Cover: Solomon's Pillars. These sandstone cliffs were carved out of the mountain by centuries of wind. They are about 15 kilometres north of Eilat, near the Timna Copper Mines. Three thousand years ago, copper was mined at Timna during the reign of King Solomon.

Previous page: Fishermen on the Sea of Galilee. The arm of the machine has a moving belt, so that the fish can go directly from the small boat to waiting lorries.

Fertile fields in the Coastal Plain. This area near Tel Aviv was once part sand dunes and part swamp. In the picture, orange groves, strawberry fields and vegetable gardens make a patchwork of colour. ▶

Contents

Shalom Israel! 4
Jerusalem 6
Landscapes and views 8
Towns and cities 10
Digging up the past 12
The passing nations 14
Making the desert bloom 16
Industry and science 18
Follow the sun 20
The kibbutz 22
People 24
Food 26
Having fun 28
Israel and the world 30
Index and summary 32

Shalom Israel!

Modern Israel is a young country but its story began over 3000 years ago. During its long history, Israel has had many names. Among them are Eretz-Yisrael (Land of Israel), Zion, the Land of Milk and Honey, Palestine, and the Holy Land.

Israel is situated in the Middle East along the eastern coastline of the Mediterranean Sea. It forms a land bridge between Asia and Africa. Israel is a small country, and has just over four million inhabitants.

Shalom!

Jews come from more than 70 different countries in the world, to make their home in Israel. They are greeted with the word, 'shalom'! Shalom means hello, goodbye and peace.

In addition to being the home of Judaism, Israel is important in the history of two other great religions: Christianity and Islam. Beautiful synagogues, churches and mosques dot the land where Moses brought the children of Israel, where Jesus taught the disciples, and where Mohammed journeyed over 1000 years ago.

Tourists and pilgrims

Since the time of the Bible, travellers and pilgrims have flocked to the Land of Israel. Today over a million tourists visit each year. They come for the archeological treasures, historic and religious sites, beautiful beaches and sunshine. Some visit the Dead Sea, the lowest place on earth. The Dead Sea is so salty that nothing can live in it – which is how it got its name. Some visitors swim in the sweet waters of Lake Kinneret, also known as the Sea of Galilee.

Buses are the easiest way to get around Israel. From Jerusalem, Israel's capital city, it is less than an hour's ride down the terraced slopes of the Judean hills to the bustling city of Tel Aviv on the Mediterranean shore.

The search for peace

Peace is very important to the future of Israel. Since Israel became an independent country in 1948, it has fought five wars with neighbouring Arab states. These states do not accept Israel's right to exist as a country because they feel that the land belongs to them. Another problem is that Palestinian Arabs who lived in this area that was once called Palestine, want to have their own state.

Israel feels that real peace will be achieved only when there are safe and accepted borders for all nations in the region. It does not believe that a Palestinian state would help to bring this about.

This disagreement is called the Arab-Israeli conflict. In 1979, a peace treaty with Egypt was signed. The search for peace ('salaam' in Arabic, 'shalom' in Hebrew) continues with other countries in the region.

LEBANON
SYRIA
Kiryat Shemona
Hulah Valley
Mt Meron
Tuval
Kfar Hanasi
Acre
Carmiel
Amiad
Haifa
Galilee
Lake Kinneret (Sea of Galilee)
Tiberias
Ein Gev
Nazareth
Hammat Gader
Coastal Plain
Caesarea
Dalyat el-Carmel
Mediterranean Sea
R. Jordan
Netanya
Herzliya
Petah Tikvah
Tel Aviv – Jaffa
Bat Yam
Ramle
Rehovot
Judean Hills
Jerusalem
Ashdod
Dead Sea
Ein Gedi
Beersheba
Arad
Massada
Dimona
NEGEV
JORDAN
Avdat
EGYPT
ARAVA
key
national borders
major cities
other cities, towns and villages
kibbutz
hills or mountains
named mountains
Lotan
Solomon's Pillars
Timna
Eilat
0
50
100 kilometres
50 miles
Red Sea

Jerusalem

Jerusalem is the capital city of modern Israel. It is the home of Parliament (which is called the 'Knesset'), the Hebrew University and 430,000 people.

Many of the houses in the city are built on the top of the hills. The parks and roads are in the valleys. There are few tall buildings in Jerusalem but graceful towers and steeples stand out against the skyline.

Old and new

Jerusalem became the capital 3000 years ago when David was King of Israel. The story of how he ruled and of the kings that came after him is told in the Bible.

Jerusalem has always been a city surrounded by walls. The walls were built with heavy stones to protect the people who lived inside. Over the centuries more than 19 different armies broke through the walls to conquer the city. Each new ruler repaired the broken walls and thought the ones he built would be the strongest. Today, most people live in the new city outside the walls.

The Knesset

The Knesset meets in Jerusalem. There are 120 members. The head of government is called the Prime Minister. There is also a President whose duties are like those of the royal family in Britain. But unlike the royal family, the President is chosen by the Members of Knesset to serve for a period of

The majestic, heavy stone walls which surround the Old City of Jerusalem.

The Knesset is the centre of government buildings in Ben-Gurion Square.

five years. Jerusalem is also the official home of the Prime Minister and the President.

A holy city

Jerusalem is a holy city. The Western Wall is the most sacred place in the world for Jews. The Wall surrounded the great Temple that was built by King Herod 2000 years ago. It is now a place of prayer.

A Jew praying at the Western Wall. Many people put notes with personal prayers into the tiny spaces between the rocks.

The Dome of the Rock stands close to the place where King Herod's Temple once stood. It was built by Moslems 1300 years ago as a monument to the prophet, Mohammed. It is known all over the world for its beautiful gold dome.

Christians come to pray at the Church of the Holy Sepulchre which holds the tomb of Jesus. The church was rebuilt by the Crusaders 800 years ago on the ruins of an earlier church.

Jerusalem is also a modern city. It has six lane highways, giant supermarkets, and luxury hotels. In the centre of the city, the outdoor shopping mall on Ben Yehudah Street is closed to cars. People stroll up and down the tree-lined avenue, shopping, or sit, sipping coffee outside cafes.

The Quarters

The first neighbourhoods in Jerusalem were inside the walls of the Old City. There are four of them so they are called 'Quarters'. In each of the Quarters – Christian, Moslem, Armenian and Jewish – you can find places of worship, schools, and open markets. The houses are made of stone and built around courtyards. The streets are also made of stone, and in some places they are so narrow that only donkeys and carts can be used for making deliveries.

When the Old City became too small for all the people who wanted to live in Jerusalem, new neighbourhoods were built outside the Walls. By law, all the buildings must be made of a stone which is a rose-gold colour, called Jerusalem stone. At sunset, the city appears to glow. That is why the city is called 'Jerusalem of Gold'.

Landscapes and views

Israel is such a small country that you can travel its length in a single day. Yet its variety of landscape and climate might make you think you've travelled the world! In one day you can find snowy mountains, subtropical valleys, deserts, farmlands, rivers and seas.

During the winter, as much as 1100 millimetres (mm) of rain may fall on Mount Meron in northern Galilee. In Eilat, the driest place in the country, the rainfall is only 15 mm during the whole year. Jerusalem has the same amount of rainfall as London, but there is one surprising difference. In London, rain falls about 300 days a year. In Jerusalem, the same amount of rain falls in about 50 days, which leaves over 300 days of warm sunshine.

The countryside

There is a narrow line of sandy shore along the coast of the Mediterranean Sea. Further inland it turns into a long stretch of fertile farmland. This area is called the Coastal Plain. Strawberries, citrus fruits, avocado pears and mangoes grow here. To the north, groves of ancient olive trees divide the mountains of Upper Galilee from the rolling hills of Lower Galilee.

The Hulah Valley is in the north-east. Older farmers who live here remember when it was a huge swamp. They worked very hard to drain it, and today they are proud of its fish ponds, cotton fields and orchards.

Perhaps the most fascinating landscapes in Israel are the desert regions of the Negev and the Arava. These are rocky areas of land

Crops growing under plastic tunnels in the Zevulon Valley near Haifa.

The 'moonscape' of the Negev. This picture is of a 'wadi' (a dry river bed) in the desert.

often marked by deep craters and tall rock pillars. Some parts of the Negev look like the surface of the moon!

Rivers and inland seas

There are many songs about the River Jordan. People sing folk songs, spirituals and hymns about this beautiful river which begins in northern Galilee and flows southward. At its source, the river is strong, but as it nears the enormous heat of the Dead Sea, it slows almost to a trickle. It is the largest river in Israel. In a country with little water, that is something to sing about.

Lake Kinneret is also known as the Sea of Galilee.

Lake Kinneret is Israel's most important source of fresh water. Around the lake there are camping sites with places to swim, fish and picnic. Once a year people come from all over the country to take part in the great swim across Lake Kinneret. Afterwards, many of the swimmers relax at the fine restaurants along the lake shore and order the favourite food of the area called St. Peter's fish.

The Dead Sea is also popular with holiday-makers. Some people come to bathe in it because the water is famous for its healing qualities. Some come just for the fun of floating on a sea which won't let you sink, even if you don't know how to swim!

Animals and plants

Israel's geography and climate have together produced a rich variety of plant and animal life. There are over 2500 different kinds of reptile, 80 types of mammal and 350 species of bird. Many of the birds only pass through Israel, stopping for a rest on their way to winter homes in Africa or summer homes in Europe. There are 280 nature reserves, and both Israelis and visitors enjoy looking at the wonders of wildlife on the hiking trails.

Towns and cities

More Israelis live in and around the city of Tel Aviv than anywhere else in the country. Surrounding the city are a number of smaller towns such as Petah Tikvah, Herzliya and Bat Yam.

Flats and homes

The tallest buildings in Israel are in Tel Aviv. The city has more hotels, shops, theatres and offices than in any other city in Israel. But less than 80 years ago, in 1909, Tel Aviv was just a tiny suburb on a sandy hill, north of the ancient port town of Jaffa. The Bible story of Jonah and the Whale begins in Jaffa.

As in other cities in Israel, most people in Tel Aviv live in modern flats. The flats are built to be as cool as possible. Floors are made of finely polished stone tiles, and windows have moveable shutters. The buildings are made of stone or of cement painted in light colours to reflect the brilliant sunshine. Each flat has its own balcony which is used for eating meals, relaxing in front of the television, or sometimes hanging clothes out to dry.

Some people live in detached houses which are called villas. Some houses are built on tall pillars which look like stilts. Using

Houses and flats crowd together in Tel Aviv. On the skyline are luxury hotels which look out on the Mediterranean Sea.

A block of flats built on pillars in Tel Aviv. Each flat has its own balcony.

pillars makes it easier to build on the hillside.

Getting around

People travel around the cities by car or bus. Sometimes people stand in a queue until the bus arrives. But once the doors open, the queue disappears as eager passengers scramble aboard in the race to find a seat.

During rush hour, cyclists can ride easily through long lines of traffic past impatient drivers who fill the air with the sounds of honking car horns.

The Sabbath

On Friday afternoon, the city streets begin to quieten down. The Jewish Sabbath, which begins at sunset and lasts until Saturday evening, is the day of rest for most Israelis. There is no public transport and shops, offices and factories are closed.

The main streets of some towns and cities are open only to pedestrians. Dizengoff Street in Tel Aviv is a favourite place to stroll and window-shop.

Dizengoff Street in Tel Aviv is famous for its shops and cafes. On the Sabbath, this street is open only to pedestrians.

New towns

The towns of Arad and Dimona in the south, Kiryat Shemona and Carmiel in the north are some of the new towns which have been built in Israel.

One reason for creating a new town is to lessen overcrowding in the big cities. Another reason is to develop new areas of the country. An advantage of a new town is that it can be carefully planned. Factories can be built in one part of the town, and houses and schools in another part, with shopping centres and parks in-between. This makes a town a pleasanter place to live in. The government offers special benefits to persuade people to move from big cities to new towns. People who live in new towns pay less taxes and can get loans to buy houses or to go into business. One of the nice things about living in these towns is the feeling of playing an important part in building a new city.

Some places in Great Britain with names from the Bible

1) Abram (Nr Manchester, England)
2) Babel (Dyfed, Wales)
3) Bethlehem (Dyfed, Wales)
4) Port Isaac (Cornwall, England)
5) Samuelston (Lothian, Scotland)
6) Saul (Nr Gloucester, England)

Digging up the past

Learning about the past

The story of how people lived thousands of years ago can often be found by exploring deep under the ground. People who look for the remains of ancient towns and villages are called archeologists. By putting together the bits and pieces that they find, archeologists show us the tools people used, the houses they lived in, the roads they walked on, the weapons they defended themselves with, and the pots they used for cooking. Sometimes archeologists find coins and jewellery and even bottles that once held perfume. Archeology is a link between the present and the past.

Visiting the past

Archeologists have found more than 3500 ancient sites in Israel. Archeology is a favourite Israeli hobby. When an important discovery is announced, people from all over the country volunteer to help dig, and schools arrange special trips so that students can join in too. Digging is hard in a hot rocky country like Israel, but the reward is the excitement of uncovering a fascinating story from the past.

The story of Massada

Almost 2000 years ago, King Herod built a fortress on top of a mountain at the edge of the Dead Sea. The name of the

Massada. On the left are the three levels of Herod's Palace. On the top, the walls which remain from rooms used for storing supplies.

mountain is Massada. About 100 years later when the Romans captured Jerusalem, nearly 1000 Jewish men, women and children refused to surrender. They remembered Massada and fled to the safety of the fortress in the desert. King Herod had built it well. Even today we can see the giant storage places, called cisterns, dug out of the rock to hold water. There were rooms for storing weapons. There were defence towers and lookout points. For three years the defenders held their own against repeated attacks. When the Romans finally broke through, they found that all the people, 960 men, women and children, had committed suicide rather than be taken into slavery by the Romans. Today Massada is a symbol of courage and freedom.

Avdat

The ancient city of Avdat stands in the heart of the Negev desert. It was built by a people called the Nabateans 2300 years ago, in order to keep watch over the camel caravans going north and south. The remains which archeologists have found show that the Nabateans were excellent farmers, traders, engineers, architects and artists. The biggest problem they had was water – there wasn't enough. They overcame the problem by saving rainwater in cisterns, very much like the ones King Herod built at Massada, but even bigger. The Nabateans also cut paths in the rock so that rainwater could flow down from the tops of the hills to their farms in the valley. They did it so well that Avdat became a garden city. Experiments are now being carried out in the Negev to test whether these methods can be used successfully in modern times.

Caesarea

In the past, Caesarea was a busy port city on the Mediterranean coast. The port is gone now, but visitors today are reminded of it when they find ancient coins and bits of pottery on the sandy beach.

The remains of a hippodrome can be seen, not far from the beach. A hippodrome is an ancient track which was used for racing horses and chariots. The hippodrome in Caesarea was built 2000 years ago by the Romans and was large enough to hold 20,000 people.

Other reminders of the past in Caesarea are the round amphitheatre that has no roof, the street of headless marble statues, and the Crusader castle with a dry moat. There are also the remains of a city wall, towers, and floors with fine mosaic pictures of beasts and birds. Caesarea's archeological treasures attract many visitors to the city every year.

The amphitheatre at Caesarea. During the Summer Festival, visiting ballet, opera and musical groups perform here. The amphitheatre was used by the Romans for games and sports.

The passing nations

The Romans

About 2000 years ago, Roman soldiers conquered Jerusalem and all the land around. Rome was then the strongest country on earth. The Romans sold the Jews into slavery or forced them to go to other countries to live. They also changed the name of Jerusalem to Aelia Capitolina and the name of the country to Palestina.

Although the name Palestina (or Palestine) is still well known, the name Aelia Capitolina has long since been forgotten.

Since then, many nations of the world have passed through the Land of Israel. Each nation came to conquer and in turn was conquered by another nation.

The Madaba Map. This 6th century Byzantine mosaic map of Jerusalem marks the Roman 'Cardo' road.

The Byzantines

Rome ruled for over 200 years. And then a new empire, Byzantium, gradually took control. The Byzantine Emperor, Constantine, and his mother, the Empress Helena, had become followers of a new religion called Christianity. They wanted all the people of Palestine to be Christian. They changed the name of the capital city, and once again called it Jerusalem.

The Arabs

Another 300 years passed, and Moslem Arabs conquered Palestine. There were three ruling families. First came the Omayyad family whose centre was in Damascus. Next was the Abasside family of

Baghdad. The third to come to power was the Fatimide family from Egypt. During this period, a new city, called Ramle, was built. Sultan Suleiman made Ramle the capital city.

The remains of a Crusader castle overlooking the Red Sea, near Eilat.

The Crusaders

The Crusaders were the next group to conquer and rule. They came from Europe in 1099. Richard the Lionheart captured the city of Acre in 1191. The Crusaders built some of their strongest forts and churches in Acre.

The Mameluke era

The Mamelukes, who had come to the Land of Israel from Egypt were the next to conquer. They destroyed almost all the ports so that the Crusaders could not attack from the sea again. They also demanded heavy taxes from the people who were already suffering because of two earthquakes and the spread of disease.

The Ottoman Turks

The Ottoman Turks ruled Palestine from 1517 until the First World War ended in 1918. In 1546 Suleiman the Magnificent rebuilt the gates and walls around Jerusalem which still stand today.

When Napoleon invaded Palestine in 1799, the Ottoman Turks, with the help of the British navy, forced him to retreat from the city of Acre. In 1918 the Ottoman Empire surrendered to British troops under the command of General Allenby.

British Rule

The League of Nations, which was made up of the countries that won the First World War, decided that Great Britain should rule Palestine. They said that British rule would last until Palestine could rule itself. Twenty-eight years later, British rule came to an end.

In May, 1948, almost 2000 years after Rome destroyed Jerusalem, the modern Jewish state of Israel was declared.

The passing nations

YEAR	CONQUEROR
70– 313	Romans
313– 636	Byzantines
637–1099	Arab-Moslems
1099–1291	Crusaders
1291–1516	Mamelukes
1517–1917	Ottoman Turks
1918–1948	British

Making the desert bloom

Over half the land in Israel is a desert called the Negev. It is not a sandy desert and although the soil of the Negev is dry and cracked, it can become good farmland if enough water is brought to it.

The National Water Carrier

The heaviest rains fall in the north. Israel's main water resources (the River Jordan and Lake Kinneret) are also in the north. The Negev desert is in the south. The Israelis had to find a method of moving the water from its low-level sources in the north up to the plateau of the southern desert.

The National Water Carrier was built in 1964 to solve this problem. It brings water from Lake Kinneret to the dry south through canals and pipelines. A chain of pumping stations lifts the water from one canal to another pushing it into tunnels that reach as far as the desert city of Beersheba.

An irrigation control unit ensures crops get enough water.

Irrigation

One of the main uses of water is for farming. When water is brought to land by channels or pipes, it is called irrigation. As more land is irrigated, the desert becomes green. Water must be used carefully. Water sprinklers throw great amounts of water into the air. Some of the water reaches the roots of the plants. But some of the water is caught on the leaves of plants and on the ground. It doesn't take long before the water dries up (evaporates) in the heat of the desert. New methods of irrigation are being developed to avoid wasting any water unnecessarily.

A drop of water in the right place is the best and most efficient way to irrigate. The 'drip' system of irrigation was invented in Israel to solve the problem of evaporation. Long plastic tubes are lined up alongside the stems of plants. Holes are made in the tube which let water drip directly to the root of

Growing plants by the drip irrigation method at Kibbutz Lotan.

the plant. A computer, which is operated by the farmer, decides how many drops of water are necessary each hour. The amount of water is based on the temperature of the air, the dryness of the soil and the type of crop which is being grown. With the drip irrigation system, plants grow stronger and faster, farming costs are lower, and less water is used.

New sources of water

It doesn't rain in Israel from May to November. This means that even in the north (where the major water sources are located) farm crops need to be irrigated during the dry season. So Israel must look for new ways of increasing the water supply.

Taking the salt out of sea water (desalination) is one possibility. Experiments have already succeeded, but the method is still so expensive that desalinated water costs too much money to use in ordinary farming. Some kinds of salt water can be mixed with fresh water and used in fish ponds and for irrigation.

Water can also be recycled. In this process, waste water which has been used in homes or factories is collected. The water passes through a series of filters and is treated with chemicals to clean and purify it. The reclaimed water can then be used again.

Rainwater is used for drinking, farming and industry. Artificial rain is created by seeding clouds. Aeroplanes fly out about 16 kilometres over the Mediterranean Sea to meet incoming clouds. They sprinkle the clouds with a mixture of chemicals. Meanwhile, on the ground, burners send a mixture of the same chemicals up into the clouds. The result is rain.

Harvesting dates in the desert. From here the dates are sent to be processed and packed.

Industry and science

Israel has a small population. In order to be successful companies, factories, or farms have to sell their products to people in other countries. This is done by making products that other countries need or want. These products are then exported.

Israel has a serious problem, however, because it does not have natural resources such as oil, iron or coal and must buy them from other countries. These imported raw materials are used to help Israel produce goods for export.

The diamond industry

Unfinished diamonds are a major import. To finish the diamonds, workers cut and polish them to create beautiful gems which are later sold in such famous department stores as Harrod's in London and Tiffany's in New York. Not all diamonds are used for jewellery. Some are industrial diamonds used in machines for cutting and drilling. Israel produces more polished and industrial diamonds than any other country in the world.

Exports

Electronic machines made in Israel are used by hospitals in many countries. The tomograph is a special x-ray machine which takes a three-dimensional photograph of the inside of a person's body. This helps doctors to discover what is wrong so that a patient can be treated correctly.

Other export products include computer parts, fashions, and plastics. Minerals called potash and bromide, mined from the Dead Sea, are also exported for use in farming.

The aircraft industry began as one small factory which only made parts for aeroplanes. Now there are many factories. They produce complete aeroplanes such as the Westwind Executive Jet.

Research and development

Research and development is what makes it possible for a country to come up with ideas for new products. Some ideas are developed in the Haifa Technion, a university that specialises in science. Research is also carried out in the laboratories of big companies that want to have more products to sell. There are 50,000 scientists and engineers in Israel. 5000 are now working on research and development. By the year 1990, this figure will have doubled.

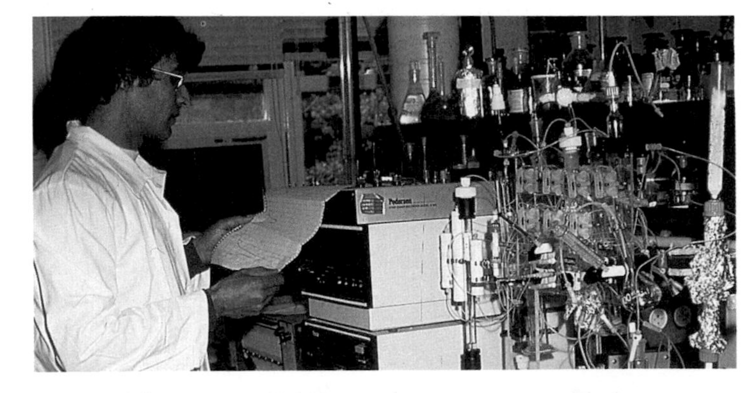

Research into new medicines being carried out in a laboratory.

Solar heating panels in use on the roof tops of buildings. Less than two hours of sunshine a day is enough to provide plenty of hot water for a family of four.

Energy

Oil is the main fuel used in Israel to operate machines and run cars. The oil is imported. The biggest single use of fuel is to make electricity. Oil is very expensive so other sources of fuel, like coal, are also used. To provide the electricity which is needed for homes and factories, three new power stations have been built. A fourth power station will be ready soon. All of these power stations use coal instead of oil.

There is one source of energy that does not have to be imported. It is the energy that comes from the sun, called solar energy. About 75 out of every 100 Israeli homes heat their water by solar energy. Each family has its own water storage tank and large glass plate (called a collector) on the roof of its house. The collector absorbs the rays of the sun and turns them into energy that heats the water in the storage tank.

New ways of storing energy from the sun are being developed. Salt water pools have been constructed, near the Dead Sea. These pools absorb and save energy from the sun's rays. The energy stored in the pools during the day is used at night to run small power plants.

Mining salt from the Dead Sea. Nearby, saltwater pools have been constructed to store energy from the sun.

Follow the sun

Some countries have coal, oil or iron as natural resources. Israel has sunshine. The sun plays an important part in making tourism one of Israel's largest industries. Over a million people visit the country every year. Out of every 100 visitors that come, 50 are from Europe, 33 are from North America and the rest from other parts of the world. Where do they find the sunshine? Everywhere.

Netanya

Sixteen settlers started the town of Netanya in 1929. They thought it would become a centre for citrus fruit growers. Soon they found the natural beauty of the city attracted many visitors. So the town was developed as a seaside resort.

Netanya sits on a cliff overlooking the Mediterranean Sea. There is a long promenade and a park with steps which lead down to the eight beaches below the city. You can usually find people on the beach because there is a warm sea breeze and gentle sun for most of the year.

Eilat

Eilat, the most southern city in Israel, is on the Red Sea. It is a busy sea port and holiday resort. Eilat has many luxury hotels, as well as simple camping sites and youth hostels.

The path from the cliff down to the seashore at Netanya. Many tourists visit this resort every year.

Big and small boats use the port at Eilat. There are many boats harboured here.

The hot springs at Hammat Gader in the Galilee. People bathe here, enjoying the relaxing effects of the warm water.

The Red Sea attracts swimmers and divers interested in the wonderful formations of coral, and the unusual tropical fish. Deep sea fishermen fish for marlin, barracuda and shark. For those who don't swim, glass-bottomed boats and an underwater museum with walls made of glass provide a clear view of this fascinating underwater world. Near Eilat are mountain trails and dry riverbeds, called 'wadis', for hikers to explore.

Visitors can also see a large desalination factory in Eilat. This is one of the largest factories where salt is removed from seawater so that it will be suitable for watering desert crops.

Tiberias

Visitors come to Tiberias especially for its water sports on Lake Kinneret. There are speed boats, water skiers, wind surfers, rowing boats and swimmers. People camp and picnic on the pebble beach that surrounds the lake. Tall palm trees, whose dates are exported to Europe, protect the picnickers from the heat of the sun. Early in the morning, fishing boats go out to bring back the day's catch. Later, the fish will be frozen and sent by truck to markets throughout the country.

South of Tiberias are natural hot springs which some people find healthy to bathe in. Many pilgrims take a dip in the water of the River Jordan at the baptismal site just south of Tiberias. Across the lake from Tiberias is Kibbutz Ein Gev. Every year, in the spring, the kibbutz holds a music festival. Musicians, singers and dancers from Israel and all over the world are invited to perform in this colourful event.

The big cities of Tel Aviv and Haifa are not typical seaside resort towns but on a sunny day their beaches are crowded. Shops are closed between one and four o'clock in the afternoon, and often people use this time for a quick swim.

Israel is working with other countries who have coastlines on the Mediterranean to protect the beaches from pollution. It is important to everyone that people have a safe and clean place to relax in the sun – as well as helping to keep the coastline and beaches beautiful.

The kibbutz

Living together

The kibbutz is a special kind of farm which is found only in Israel. The word 'kibbutz' means 'come together', and that is how the people on kibbutz live. They work together, eat together and celebrate holidays together.

People who live on kibbutz don't need money to pay for their houses, or for groceries. They don't pay for clothing either, or for books or toys. This is because people on kibbutz work as hard as they can and in return get as much as they need. Many countries send students and teachers to learn about this sharing way of life.

There are over 260 kibbutz farms all over Israel. Some are large with 1000 people or more. Some are small with less than 100 'kibbutzniks' (the name for people who live on kibbutz).

The best known kibbutz crops are cotton, avocado pears, oranges, bananas and mangoes. The kibbutzniks raise chickens and turkeys and breed fish in specially constructed ponds.

Unlike farms in other countries, kibbutz farms also have factories. They make everything from plastic bags to computers, from shoes to furniture.

The children's house

Children on the kibbutz live a special life. From the time they are babies they spend the day with other children of their own age in a children's house while their parents are at work. The house has a playroom and a garden, a bedroom, a small kitchen, and a classroom. At school, they call their teachers by their first names because the teachers are

Kibbutz fields. Green crops are flourishing next to newly ploughed areas of brown earth.

Young children in the classroom of a kibbutz children's house. Lessons are held from Sunday to Friday.

Breakfast in a kibbutz dining room. Some of these kibbutzniks will have already done several hours work on the kibbutz, before sitting down to their meal.

kibbutzniks too. When school is finished for the day, the children take care of the animals and plants on the children's farm.

When they are 13, children move out of their parents' home and into small houses nearby which they share with friends of their own age. At about the age of 18, they can become adult members of the kibbutz.

The dining hall

Kibbutzniks eat their meals together. That is why the dining hall is the largest building on the kibbutz, much larger than most restaurants. After getting up very early in the morning and perhaps working in the fields or factories, kibbutz members eat a breakfast that has been prepared by kibbutzniks who work in the kitchen. After breakfast other kibbutzniks will be busy washing dishes and planning lunch. Mealtimes are a very important part of kibbutz life. Although every home has a small kitchen and members can cook at home if they wish, kibbutzniks usually choose to eat together as one large family in the dining hall.

The general meeting

Once a week, on a Saturday evening, the members of kibbutz gather in the dining hall. This time it is not to eat. It is for the General Meeting. Decisions have to be made on how to run the kibbutz. Kibbutzniks set the rules for their community, elect leaders and decide how to spend the money they have earned. Should they build a new school building? Should they buy a television set for each family? Is it time for a new tractor? Each person has a chance to speak, and at the end of the meeting a vote is taken. The kibbutz is a democracy.

Volunteers

You don't have to be an Israeli to live on a kibbutz. You can go as a volunteer for a few months and share in kibbutz life. Volunteers come from all over the world and work in all parts of the kibbutz. Some come from Great Britain. Often they choose to go to kibbutz farms such as Kfar Hanasi, Amiad or Tuval where many of the kibbutz members are from Britain. Most volunteers find life on a kibbutz hard work, but fun too!

People

Many different peoples live in Israel. There are Jews, Arabs (Christian and Moslem), Druze and Bedouin. In addition to Hebrew which is the most widely used language, people also speak other languages and have different customs.

The Jews

Most of the people who live in Israel are Jews. Some Jews have always lived here but 100 years ago more began coming back in large numbers. They came back to rebuild the Jewish country that had been conquered by the Romans almost 2000 years before. During that time Jews remembered and prayed to return to their country. The return of the Jews to Israel is called Zionism.

The two largest groups of Jews are Sephardi and Ashkenasi. Sephardi Jews come from the Mediterranean area and from Arabic speaking countries. Ashkenasi Jews come from European and other Western countries.

The Bnei-Yisrael Jews come from India. They tell how their forefathers were shipwrecked near Bombay over 2000 years ago.

The Jews of Yemen were flown into Israel in 1949 and 1950. This seemed to fulfil the promise in the Bible: 'I will bring you back on the wings of eagles'.

In 1985, the name 'Operation Moses' was given to the airlift which brought thousands of Jews from Ethiopia to Israel.

The Jewish ceremony of 'Bar Mitzvah' when a 13-year-old boy accepts the commandments of Jewish religious law.

The Arabs

Arabic is the first language of Israeli Arabs. There are five daily newspapers published in Arabic, and there are Arabic programmes every day on television.

Until recently most Arabs were farmers. Now, more and more Arabs live and work in the cities. Even though most Israeli Arabs dress in modern, western clothes, the 'khaffiyeh' is still popular. A 'khaffiyeh' is a cloth head covering, sometimes held in place by a round black rope called an 'akkal'.

Arab markets are filled with fruit and vegetables and large round trays stacked with delicious sweetcakes made of honey and nuts. The shops have gold jewellery, pottery and copper. Arab hospitality is well known and visitors are sure to be invited to share a small cup of thick, sweet Turkish coffee.

The Druze and the Bedouin

The Druze were once Moslems. Eight hundred years ago they formed their own religion. There are 18 Druze villages in the Galilee. The largest and most colourful is Dalyat el-Carmel. The Druze of Israel are hard working farmers. They grow olives and grapes. They also farm most of the tobacco grown in Israel even though their religion forbids them to smoke!

In some ways the life of the Bedouin is the same as it was in ancient days. The people are divided into tribes. Many still travel with their sheep in search of water and pasture land.

But times are changing and modern influences are forcing the Bedouin into different ways. Children go to school. More and more Bedouin are becoming farmers. Many Bedouin people have moved into houses instead of living in goat-skin tents.

One tradition that is still strong is the Bedouin market on Thursday mornings in the city of Beersheba. Embroidered dresses, decorated mirrors and sheepskin coats are on sale alongside plastic buckets and metal pans.

(*Above*) An Arab market. (*Below*) A Bedouin woman.

א ב ג ד ה ו ז ח ט י כ

New words from old

Hebrew is a very old language. It was spoken by the Jewish people during the time of the Bible. Hebrew is also the language of modern Israel. Often new words had to be created for objects that didn't exist long ago in the days of King David. Here are some examples:

mee-lah means word. So, *mee-lone* is a dictionary.

et is the word for time. *E-tone* means newspaper.

sha-ah is the word for hour. So, *sha-one* was created to mean clock.

kole means voice, and *no-ah* means move.
So, *kole-no-ah* is a film that you see in a cinema.

re-mez is signal, and *or* is light. So, *ramz-or* is a traffic light.

ל מ נ ס ע פ צ ק ר שׁ ת*

* The Hebrew alphabet.

Food

Food, glorious food! Whether they buy it in the open market, at the supermarket, at a fast food stand on the street or along the sea shore, Israelis enjoy food. Fresh fruit and vegetables of all kinds are an important part of the family menu. Hot, flaky 'bourekas' (a pastry pie filled with either salty cheese, spinach or mashed, spiced potatoes) and 'blintzes' (thin pancakes usually filled with cheese or jam and served with cream or apple sauce) are favourite choices.

In Israel the day begins early. Schools and offices begin work at eight o'clock in the morning. By ten o'clock, people are ready for tea and biscuits and sometimes a sandwich. This snack is called 'the ten o'clock meal'. There is also a 'four o'clock meal', much like afternoon tea in Britain.

Varieties of olives, fruit and fish being sold in the Carmel market in Tel Aviv.

A Jerusalem family sharing a Sabbath meal on Friday evening.

Pocketful of pitta

'Pitta' is a flat, thin circle of bread, sometimes with a 'pocket' in it. It is a handy food because you can wrap it around all kinds of snacks or you can stuff snacks into the 'pocket'. 'Houmous' and 't'hina' are favourite stuffers. Houmous is a thickish paste made of ground chickpeas and sharp spices. T'hina is a sauce made of ground sesame seeds with olive oil and parsley. Sometimes the ground chickpeas are made into little balls and fried in hot, sizzling oil. Three or four of the balls in a pitta pocket, together with cucumber, lettuce and tomato, smothered in t'hina sauce and just a pinch of hot pepper, makes the famous 'falafel'! When pitta is wrapped around thin slices of grilled lamb, it is called 'shwarma'.

Snacks

Eating while walking along is one way that busy Israelis keep on the go. Sweet and juicy corn on the cob is a treat. Stalls with huge pans full of boiling water keep the corn simmering for sunbathers at the beach, for children on the way home from school, and for late night strollers after the cinema.

'Garinim' are seeds – sunflower seeds, pumpkin seeds, watermelon seeds – all kinds of seeds that are roasted and salted. Sometimes the seeds are mixed with nuts like cashews, pistachios, almonds and hazelnuts. Like crisps, they are eaten everywhere: on the street, at a football match, and in front of the television.

A foodstall selling aubergines, sweet peppers and other delicacies.

Roadside markets

Strawberries like sandy soil and lots of sunshine. They find both in Israel. From late winter onwards strawberries are exported to markets in Europe. In Israel they are sold in big city supermarkets and in small town food shops. The freshest and cheapest berries come from the roadside stalls set up near the farms on which they are grown. Large, colourful sun umbrellas attract buyers driving past. There are no fancy boxes or packages with labels, just big red ripe strawberries sold by the pound.

Late spring and summer is the melon season. Honeydew, cantaloupe and especially watermelons are piled high for sale in open sheds. The sheds are put up along city streets and motorways just for the period of the melon season. At night, when other businesses close, lights strung up on the shed are turned on, and the melon sellers keep on working.

How to grow your own avocado tree

1. Cut an avocado pear in half lengthways, remove the stone.
2. Take the stone and wash it well.
3. Push 4 cocktail sticks (or wooden matches) into the stone around its middle.
4. Fill a glass with lukewarm water. Place the stone with the round end in the water, supported by the sticks. (See diagram.)
5. WAIT.

****

It can take two months for the stone to split. Then a thick, whitish root will appear. Keep the plant in a well lit place, but out of direct sunlight.

When the trunk is about 8 centimetres high, put it into a proper pot. Leave part of the stone showing.

Unfortunately your avocado plant won't start to produce avocados until it's about seven years old and over nine metres high!

Having fun

Children in Israel go to school six days a week. Their parents work six days a week too. What do they do on their days off?

Sports

Outdoor sports are a favourite way to spend free time. There is tennis and swimming, wind surfing and snorkelling. The most popular sports are basketball and football. Basketball and football teams play before crowds of loyal fans. During the European Cup Championships, in 1977 and 1981, huge outdoor television screens were placed in the square next to City Hall in Tel Aviv so that thousands of excited fans could watch the games together. When the Israel basketball team won, the crowds celebrated the victory by waving flags, honking car horns and dancing in the streets throughout the night.

Picnicking, backpacking and hiking are also popular. Schoolchildren go on overnight hikes with their classes and teachers to explore the mountains, valleys, deserts and streams. They pitch tents and cook over camp fires, sometimes spending a whole week out-of-doors.

Music and dance

Israelis enjoy going to concerts. There are five major orchestras in the country. The Israeli Philharmonic Orchestra is the oldest and most well-known. It performs over 200 concerts a year. The Mann Auditorium in Tel Aviv and Binyanei Ha-U'ma in Jerusalem are the largest concert halls in Israel. Each hall can seat 3000 people.

There are three modern dance companies and many smaller dance groups. The 'Kol U'Demama' (sound and silence) dance group is made up of both deaf and hearing dancers.

Wind surfing is a favourite water sport.

The Israeli Philharmonic Orchestra performing in Tel Aviv.

The dancers who can hear the music give signals that are part of the dance steps to the deaf dancers. Through the floor, the deaf dancers can feel the vibrations made by the music and by the other dancers. These signals tell them what the next movement should be. During a performance you cannot tell who is a deaf dancer and who is a hearing dancer.

Theatre and cinema

The national theatre of Israel is called 'Habimah' (The Stage). There are four other large theatre companies. They perform plays written in Hebrew and plays which have been translated from other languages.

There is a large film centre in Jerusalem called the Cinemateque. It has over 3500 films, a film library, and halls for viewing films. Sometimes, at a special showing, the Cinemateque invites the writer, director or an actor in the film to talk to the audience about how the film was made.

The Jerusalem Theatre is a centre for music and dance performances. Street players often perform in the open courtyard of the building.

Books and reading

The United Nations wanted to know about the reading habits of people in different countries. So they asked questions in bookshops and libraries, book clubs and schools. They found out that Israelis read and publish more books per person than other countries with a similar population. One in every four people in Israel reads at least one book a month.

Every two years there is an International Book Fair in Jerusalem where publishers display their new books. There are books for children, books on photography, story books and cookbooks to name but a few. There are books in French, German, Italian and English, and of course, Hebrew and Arabic. Every Spring, there is a Hebrew Book Week. Parks and street corners become crowded book markets as tables and lights are set up to sell books at special sale prices.

Special annual events

Israel Festival, Jerusalem

Tel Aviv Spring Festival

Festival of Alternative Theatre, Acre

Ein Gev Music Festival

Kinneret Festival

Children's Hebrew Song Festival

Liturgica Week, Jerusalem

Christian Choir Assembly, Jerusalem

International Folklore Festival, Haifa

Hassidic Song Festival

Israel Jazz Festival

Israel Film Festival

International Puppet Theatre

Zimria – Assembly of Choirs

Arthur Rubinstein Piano Competition

International Harp Contest

Hebrew Book Week

International Book Fair, Jerusalem

Israel and the world

People all over the world know about Israel even though they may never have been there. This is because of the Bible. From the Bible we know about Noah and his ark, Moses and the ten commandments, the mighty kings, David and Solomon, the story of Ruth, and Jesus of Nazareth. The Bible is holy to the Jewish and Christian religions. Some of the people in the Bible such as Noah, Abraham and Moses are also honoured in Islam, the Moslem religion.

The EEC

In the days of the Bible, King Solomon traded perfume from the oasis of Ein Gedi and copper from the mines of Timna for spices, gold and precious stones from the Queen of Sheba of Ethiopia.

Today, Israel's major trading partners are the countries which are members of the European Economic Community (the EEC). Israel is not a full member of the Community, but it has a special agreement with the EEC. Under this agreement, people in Europe do not have to pay import duties on certain Israeli products.

Israel has almost the same kind of agreement with the United States. It is called a free trade agreement. There are also special trade agreements with Australia, Austria, Canada, Japan, Finland, New Zealand, Norway, Sweden and Switzerland.

Sharing ideas

Most countries try to find ways of providing their citizens with a better way of life. New

Jaffa oranges are a major product exported to Europe from Israel through the EEC.

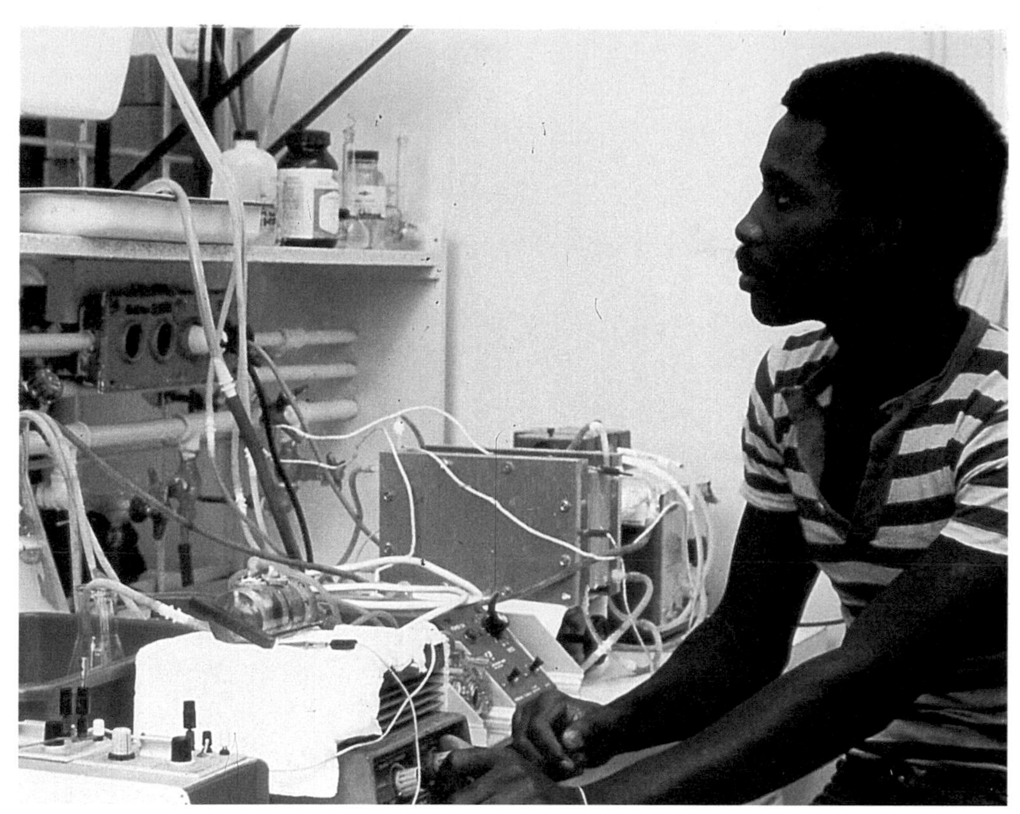

A visiting scientist from Africa doing research at the Weizmann Institute in Rehovot. Hundreds of overseas scientists visit the Institute every year.

The Israeli flag

countries are especially interested in learning from each other how to do this.

For over 30 years, Israel has been sharing its ideas and information with other developing countries around the world. During this time, more than 27,000 men and women have come to Israel to study. They come from Asia, Africa and Latin America. They learn about new methods in farming, medicine, housing, education and science. Nine thousand Israeli experts have gone abroad to work on special projects in other countries. They work on new systems for controlling water and irrigation, and also build bridges.

Going into Space

Israel is now developing its first space satellite. A satellite travels around the Earth in space. It receives and sends messages between places on Earth. At first, Israeli scientists and engineers worked on space research in their laboratories. Later, projects were carried out with the help of satellites sent into space by NASA (National Aeronautics and Space Administration), the U.S. Space Agency.

The satellites provide information that is used in agricultural planning and in fishing. One satellite project is making a survey of citrus groves. Another project will study the evaporation process in the Dead Sea.

The Israeli satellite is a communication satellite. It will be some 22,000 miles in space above Algeria, and it will remain in the same position in what is called a stationary orbit. One of the uses of the satellite will be to increase the number of television channels and telephone lines available to people in Israel.

Index and summary

Africa 4, 9, 31
Akkal 24
Arabic 29
Arabs 4, 14–15, 24–25
Archeology 4, 12–13
Arts 13, 21, 28–29
Asia 4, 31

Bar Mitzvah 24
Bedouin 24, 25
Beersheba 16, 25
Bible 6, 10, 11, 24, 30
Books 29

Caesarea 13
Children 22–23, 27, 28
Christians 4, 7, 14, 29, 30

Dead Sea 4, 9, 18, 19, 31
Deserts 8–9, 13, 16, 21
Diamonds 18
Druze 24, 25

EEC 30
Egypt 4
Eilat 8, 20–21
Energy, sources of 18, 19, 20
Ethiopia 24
Europe 15, 21, 27, 30

Factories 17, 21, 22, 23
Falafel 26
Farms 16, 17, 22, 23, 25
Fish 8, 9, 21, 22, 31
Flag 31
Fruit 8, 22, 25, 26, 27, 30

Government 6–7, 11
Great Britain 8, 11, 15, 23, 26

Haifa 21
Hebrew 24, 25, 29
History 4, 7, 12–13, 14–15, 24
Holidays 20–21, 22
Homes 6, 7, 10, 23, 25
Houmous 26

Irrigation 16–17, 31

Jerusalem 4, 6–7, 8, 14, 29
Jews 4, 7, 13, 14, 24
Jordan, River 9, 16, 21

Khaffiyeh 24
Kibbutz 21, 22–23
Kinneret, Lake 4, 9, 16, 21
Knesset 6

Markets 7, 25, 27
Massada 12
Mediterranean Sea 4, 8, 10, 20
Moslems 7, 14, 24–25, 30
Mount Meron 8

National Water Carrier 16
Netanya 20

Palestine 4, 14, 15
Pitta 26
Pollution 21

Red Sea 15, 20, 21
Religion 4, 7, 14, 24

Sabbath 11
Salt 17, 19, 21
School 7, 22–23, 26, 28
Sea of Galilee 4, 9, 16, 21
Seaside resorts 20–21
Shwarma 26
Space 31
Sports 21, 27, 28

Tel Aviv 4, 10, 11, 21, 28
T'hina 26
Tiberias 21
Tourism 4, 20

United Nations 29
United States 30

Western Wall 7

Area:	22,000 square kilometres
Population:	4,266,200
Capital:	Jerusalem
Main towns:	Tel Aviv-Jaffa, Haifa, Beersheba, Eilat
Main exports:	Electronics, polished diamonds, agricultural products
Main imports:	Fuels, raw materials
Main crops:	Cotton, citrus fruits, avocado pears, tomatoes, strawberries, melons
Highest point:	Mount Meron, 1208 metres
Longest river:	River Jordan, 299 kilometres
Official languages:	Hebrew, Arabic
Currency:	100 agorot to 1 shekel
National airline:	El Al